HERBERT HOOVER
THE UNCOMMON MAN

Contents

Published by the Hoover Presidential Library Association, Inc., August 1974, Copyright 1974.

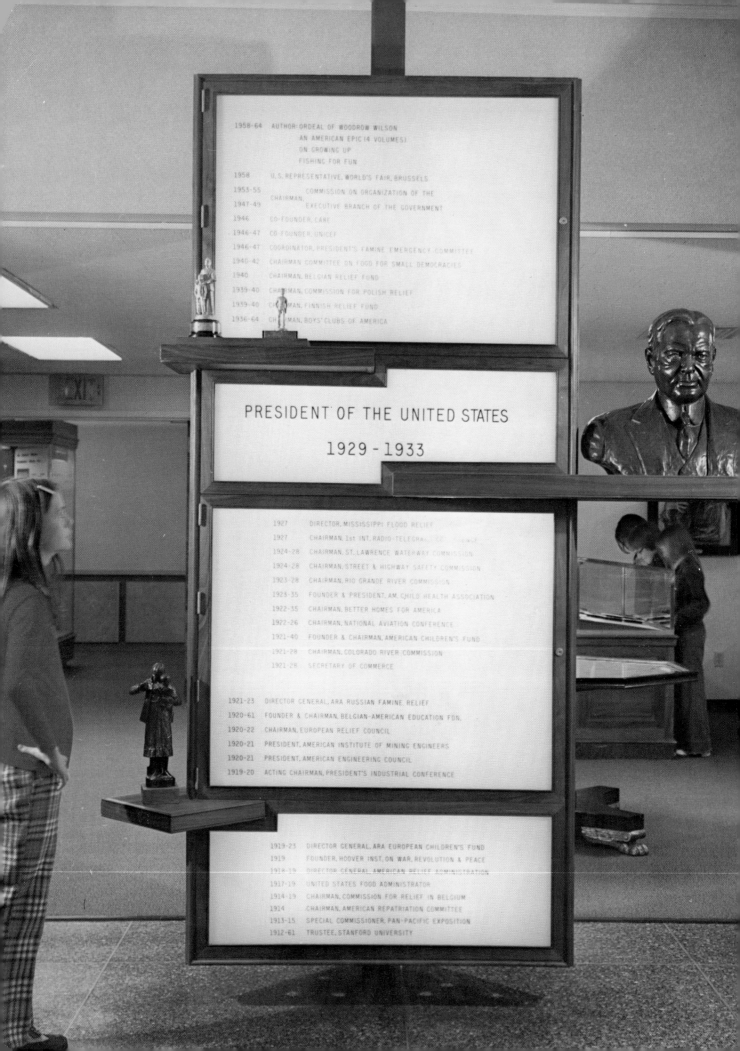

1958-64   AUTHOR:ORDEAL OF WOODROW WILSON
                AN AMERICAN EPIC (4 VOLUMES)
                ON GROWING UP
                FISHING FOR FUN
1958   U.S. REPRESENTATIVE, WORLD'S FAIR, BRUSSELS
1953-55   COMMISSION ON ORGANIZATION OF THE
           CHAIRMAN,
1947-49   EXECUTIVE BRANCH OF THE GOVERNMENT
1946   CO-FOUNDER, CARE
1946-47   CO-FOUNDER, UNICEF
1946-47   COORDINATOR, PRESIDENT'S FAMINE EMERGENCY COMMITTEE
1940-42   CHAIRMAN, COMMITTEE ON FOOD FOR SMALL DEMOCRACIES
1940   CHAIRMAN, BELGIAN RELIEF FUND
1939-40   CHAIRMAN, COMMISSION FOR POLISH RELIEF
1939-40   CHAIRMAN, FINNISH RELIEF FUND
1936-64   CHAIRMAN, BOYS' CLUBS OF AMERICA

PRESIDENT OF THE UNITED STATES

1929 - 1933

1927   DIRECTOR, MISSISSIPPI FLOOD RELIEF
1927   CHAIRMAN, 1st INT. RADIO-TELEGRAPH CONFERENCE
1924-28   CHAIRMAN, ST. LAWRENCE WATERWAY COMMISSION
1924-28   CHAIRMAN, STREET & HIGHWAY SAFETY COMMISSION
1923-28   CHAIRMAN, RIO GRANDE RIVER COMMISSION
1923-35   FOUNDER & PRESIDENT, AM. CHILD HEALTH ASSOCIATION
1922-35   CHAIRMAN, BETTER HOMES FOR AMERICA
1922-26   CHAIRMAN, NATIONAL AVIATION CONFERENCE
1921-40   FOUNDER & CHAIRMAN, AMERICAN CHILDREN'S FUND
1921-28   CHAIRMAN, COLORADO RIVER COMMISSION
1921-28   SECRETARY OF COMMERCE

1921-23   DIRECTOR GENERAL, ARA RUSSIAN FAMINE RELIEF
1920-61   FOUNDER & CHAIRMAN, BELGIAN-AMERICAN EDUCATION FDN.
1920-22   CHAIRMAN, EUROPEAN RELIEF COUNCIL
1920-21   PRESIDENT, AMERICAN INSTITUTE OF MINING ENGINEERS
1920-21   PRESIDENT, AMERICAN ENGINEERING COUNCIL
1919-20   ACTING CHAIRMAN, PRESIDENT'S INDUSTRIAL CONFERENCE

1919-23   DIRECTOR GENERAL, ARA EUROPEAN CHILDREN'S FUND
1919   FOUNDER, HOOVER INST. ON WAR, REVOLUTION & PEACE
1918-19   DIRECTOR GENERAL, AMERICAN RELIEF ADMINISTRATION
1917-19   UNITED STATES FOOD ADMINISTRATOR
1914-19   CHAIRMAN, COMMISSION FOR RELIEF IN BELGIUM
1914   CHAIRMAN, AMERICAN REPATRIATION COMMITTEE
1913-15   SPECIAL COMMISSIONER, PAN-PACIFIC EXPOSITION
1912-61   TRUSTEE, STANFORD UNIVERSITY

The Early Years

1874 - 1914

Ancestry

The Hoover family emigrated to America about 1738. Andreas Huber, a young man of Swiss ancestry, joined two older brothers in Pennsylvania. In Europe the Hubers held pietists beliefs. This probably prepared them for their membership in the Society of Friends. Andreas married and bought land in North Carolina where he established a grist mill and prosperous farm. Because of the slavery issue, the Hoovers migrated to a Quaker settlement in Ohio. Herbert Hoover's father and grandfather were among the Hoovers who left Ohio in 1854 for the prairie lands of Iowa. They settled in the small town of West Branch and established farms.

JESSE CLARK HOOVER
- B. 1846 West Milton, Ohio
- D. 1880 West Branch, Iowa

ELI HOOVER
- B. 1820 Miami County, Ohio
- D. 1892 Hardin County, Iowa

JESSE HOOVER
- B. 1800 Randolph Co., North Carolina
- D. 1856 West Branch, Iowa

JOHN HOOVER
- B. 1760 Near Uniontown, Maryland
- D. 1831 West Milton, Ohio

ANDREAS HUBER — (ANDREW HOOVER)
- B. 1723 Oberkulm, Switzerland
- D. 1794 Uwharie, Randolph Co., North Carolina

GREGOR JONAS HUBER
- B. 1668 Oberkulm, Switzerland
- D. 1741 Ellerstadt, Palatinate (Germany)

JOHANN HEINRICH HUBER
- B. 1644 Oberkulm, Switzerland
- D. 1706 Oberkulm, Switzerland

Right: "The Huber home in Oberkulm, Switzerland."

"Four generations of Hoovers gathered for this family photo in West Branch, Iowa, 1878."

4

Jesse Hoover, the village blacksmith, and his wife Hulda became the parents of a new son, August 10, 1874. They named him Herbert Hoover.

His early years in West Branch were filled with many joys, but there were also many sorrows.

"As gentle as are the memories of those times, I am not recommending a return to the good old days. Sickness was greater, and death came sooner."

When "Bertie" was six years old, his father caught a cold which worsened rapidly. On December 13, 1880, Jesse Clark Hoover died from "Rheumatism of the Heart" at the age of 34.

As a help to Hulda Hoover, an uncle, who was an Indian Agent on the Osage Reservation in Oklahoma, took Herbert to live with him. The following summer Herbert lived with another uncle in Sioux County, Iowa.

"We lived in a sod house and I was privileged to ride the lead horse of a team which was opening the virgin soil."

Early in 1884, tragedy struck again. Returning home from a Friends Meeting in Muscatine, Iowa, Hulda Hoover was caught in a winter storm. She developed a severe cold, "which rapidly grew worse, in much the same way as did my father." On February 24, 1884, she died of typhoid fever and pneumonia.

Following the death of Hulda Hoover, the little home was parentless. Herbert was taken into the family of his uncle, Allen Hoover, who farmed north of West Branch.

Above: "Hulda Randall Minthorn was born in Ontario, Canada, in 1848. When Hulda was eleven, her family immigrated to West Branch, Iowa, where she grew up. She taught school before her marriage to Jesse Hoover in 1870."

"Jesse Clark Hoover was born near West Milton, Ohio, in 1846, and moved with his family to West Branch in 1854. A hard worker, Jesse ran a blacksmith shop until 1879, when he established a profitable farm implement business."

Oregon

In 1885, Uncle Henry John Minthorn and his wife lost their only son. They asked that Herbert be sent to live with them. Uncle Allen found a family emmigrating to Oregon who agreed to take the boy along. On November 12, 1885, the following news item appeared in the West Branch *Local Record*:

"Mr. and Mrs. O. T. Hammel and Bertie Hoover started on their long journey Tuesday evening."

Upon his arrival in Newberg, Oregon, Herbert was enrolled in Pacific Academy (Quaker) where his uncle was the school principal. Three years later the Minthorn family moved to Salem and Herbert went to work as an office boy for his uncle. He taught himself typing, and attended night school to learn "higher" mathematics. Among the visitors to his uncle's office was an engineer from the East who impressed upon him the importance of a college education and introduced him to the profession of engineering.

Stanford University

When Stanford University opened in 1891, Herbert Hoover entered the Department of Geology. He supported himself by working as a "typist". During summer vacations, he was employed by the U.S. Geological Survey in the deserts and mountains of Nevada and California. On campus, he was the financial manager for the football team and arranged the first "Big Game" between Stanford and the University of California. With friends, he organized a group called the "Barbarians" to run against the fraternities for class offices. The "Barbarians" were victorious, and Herbert Hoover became the first non-fraternity man to hold an office in the student government.

Above: "The Minthorn home in Newberg, Oregon."

Left: "Uncle Henry John Minthorn in 1920."

Engineering Career Begins

When Herbert Hoover graduated in 1895, he had "forty dollars in my pocket, and no debts." His first job as a graduate engineer was pushing an ore cart in a California mine for 20¢ an hour on a ten-hour shift, seven days a week. After a few months he obtained a second job as a "driller" with full miner's wages. By Christmas he had saved $100, so he traveled to Berkeley to spend the holidays with his brother, Theodore, and his younger sister, May.

During this visit, Hoover obtained a job interview with Louis Janin, a prominent San Francisco mining consultant. Although the only available job was that of a typist, Hoover accepted it. Impressed with the knowledge and initiative of the young engineer-typist, Janin assigned him to more responsible tasks. In 1897, Janin recommended the 23-year-old Hoover to the British mining firm, Bewick Moreing Co., to manage their Australian mining properties. Hoover bought a new suit of clothes, grew a beard to make himself appear older, and set out for Australia.

CHINA

Hoover's work took him away for long periods of time on journeys throughout China. Mrs. Hoover took advantage of his absence to learn the Chinese language and to begin a collection of Chinese porcelains. Their sojourn was interrupted in June 1900 when they came under artillery fire in Tientsin, China, at the outbreak of the Boxer Rebellion.

Marriage

During his senior year at Stanford, Herbert Hoover met Miss Lou Henry, a freshman from Iowa who was majoring in Geology. In 1899, after two years in Australia, Bewick Moreing offered Hoover a more responsible job in China. He proposed by cable to Miss Henry. They were married February 10, 1899, in Monterey, California, and sailed for China. Lou Henry's mother, Mrs. Charles Henry, described her feelings about Hoover in a letter:

"He had never been to the house but once. Had dinner with us before he went to Australia. We had made up our minds not to like him very well as he was going to take Lou so far away, but after he had been here a few days ... I think we all liked him about as much as Lou did ... Lou met him first at Stanford very soon after she entered ... He took her to her first party there. He graduated that year, was at Stanford at times the next year as he would have laboratory work to do ...

When they wanted to know if he would go to China he said he would if they gave him time to go to the United States first. So he came all that distance — just to get Lou — had no other business whatever."

International Engineering

In 1901 Hoover was made a partner in Bewick Moreing Co., and during the next eight years he circled the globe five times in his capacity of mining engineer. Mrs. Hoover accompanied him on most of his travels. (When their children were born, the entire family travelled together. Mrs. Hoover carried the babies in a basket.) Herbert Hoover, Jr. was born in London, August 4, 1903. Five weeks later he sailed with his parents to Australia. Allan was born in London, July 17, 1907. Five weeks later he too, was in a basket, bound for Burma.

Hoover established his own firm of mining consultants in 1908. By this time he had established an international reputation as a "doctor of sick mines". His success as a mining engineer stemmed from a principle evident throughout his entire career — "Elimination of Waste."

HOOVER'S INTERNATIONAL ENGINEERING
1909-1914
1909 *United States, England, Germany, Poland, Russia, China*
1910 *United Staes, Scotland, England, France, Russia, Burma, Korea, Japan*
1911 *United States, Great Britain, Belgium, Germany, Russia, Burma*
1912 *United States, Great Britain, France, Italy, Russia*
1913 *United States, Canada, Belgium, Germany, Russia*
1914 *United States, Great Britain, France, Italy, Belgium, Holland, Germany*
Offices in New York, San Francisco, London, Petrograd, Paris

TOMMYKNOCKER
"The tommyknockers were the gnomes who for centuries had given benevolent aid to the hard rock miners, mostly by warning of rock falls and water breaks. They were associated with fairies, generally, and we all believe in fairies.

"They had a long record with the happiness of the miners ...I had occasion to meet the mining gnomes in person in a Russian mine. The Russian miners so believed in them that they cast life-size figures of them in the machine shops and placed them in needed spots around and in the mines.

"To prove my belief in their efficacy, I brought one of them home, although he weighs many pounds. He still guards the entrance to my apartment in the Waldorf-Astoria."

Herbert Hoover to Joseph Milliken
May 20, 1963

DE RE METALLICA
One of the significant contributions of Mr. and Mrs. Hoover to mining engineering was the translation of the **De Re Metallica,** *a Latin mining text of the Sixteenth Century still used as a standard reference work. The task took the Hoovers five years, from 1907-1912.*

Philosophy

Hoover's success in mine management was due to his views on elimination of waste, equal opportunity, and voluntarism. Hoover thought voluntarism could produce more than coercion, so his miners worked shorter hours at higher wages than his competitors. Ability and dependability were the sole criteria by which he chose men for positions of responsibility. When lecturing at Columbia University in 1908, he shocked many with his opinions:

"Labor unions ... are normal and proper antidotes for unlimited capitalistic organizations."

"The time when the employer could ride roughshod over his labor is disappearing with the doctrine of laissez faire *upon which it was founded."*

"No administrator begrudges a division with his men of the increased profit arising from increased efficiency."

World War I
Public Service Begins

World War I Begins

When World War I began in August 1914, Hoover was in his London office. Thousands of American tourists were stranded in Europe with little ready cash and no credit. They converged on London and demanded assistance from the American Ambassador, Walter Hines Page. Page called on Hoover for help. Along with other American engineers, he set up an *ad hoc* tourist bureau and private bank to provide emergency credit. In addition, neutral ships were chartered to transport more than 120,000 tourists to America. In all, more than $1 million was loaned on personal checks and I.O.U.'s. This rescue venture lost only $300.

In October 1914, just as Hoover was about to sail for America, Belgian Representatives came to Ambassador Page seeking help for the people of Brussels, who were on the verge of starvation. Again, Page called on Hoover. For three days, Hoover, Page and the Belgians discussed the problems and explored possible solutions. It was clear to Hoover that a personal

commitment to the Belgian cause would have severe consequences on his personal life, his business, and his fortune. During those three nights, Hoover pondered his decision. On the fourth morning he came to breakfast with his friend and house guest, Will Irwin, who later reported:

"He bade me good-morning, poured and sweetened his coffee, looked up, and said, 'Well, let the fortune go to hell.'"

With that phrase the Commission for Relief in Belgium came to life and a completely new course for Hoover's life was charted.

Commission for Relief in Belgium

Through four years of warfare, the Commission fed 11 million people in Belgium and Northern France. More than $1 billion was collected to finance the relief operations, and efficient administration kept the overhead costs below one-half of one per cent. Following liquidation of the C.R.B., the remaining funds were used for restoration of libraries in Belgium and for establishment of

Above: "The Hoovers say farewell as Mrs. Hoover and the boys prepare to sail to America."

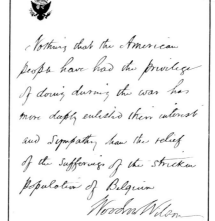

Nothing that the American people have had the privilege of doing during the war has more deeply enlisted their interest and sympathy than the relief of the sufferings of the stricken population of Belgium

Woodrow Wilson

the Belgian-American Educational Foundation.

On January 12, 1915, three months after the C.R.B. was established, Ambassador Page wrote to President Woodrow Wilson:

"Life is worth more, too, for knowing Hoover, But for him Belgium would now be starved ..."

Children were the main concern of the C.R.B. and food kitchens were established in the schools where a supplementary "hot lunch" was served to children and to pregnant and nursing mothers. The children of Belgium were healthier after the war than before. Hot lunch programs were later introduced in American schools through the American Child Health Association.

FLOUR SACKS

In a time of need the Belgian people found a beautiful way to express their gratitude. The sacks containing flour from American and Canadian millers for the C.R.B. food shipments were decorated with intricate embroidery or hand paintings and returned by the Belgians to Mr. Hoover. Designed and made by housewives and school children, the sacks proclaimed "merci aux Americains" and " hommage de gratitude" amid colorful designs of Belgian and American flags, bouquets of flowers, and the Belgian lion. Also, some sacks were used to make clothing, suitcases, folding screens, and boxes.

FRIEND OF THE BELGIAN PEOPLE

Herbert Hoover felt that foreign decorations were not suitable for the representative of a democratic government. When Hoover refused to accept any kind of honor or decoration from the Belgian government, King Albert created a new order titled "Friend of the Belgian People" which would have only one member — Herbert Hoover.

"In Belgium, *by Louis Raemaekers.*"

Life is worth more, too, for knowing Hoover. But for him Belgium would now be starved, however generously people may have given food. He's gathering together & transporting & getting distributed $5,000,000 worth a month, with a perfect organization of volunteers, chiefly American. He has a fleet of 35 ships, flying the Commission's flag— the only flag that all belligerents have entered into an agreement to respect and to defend. He came to me the other day & said, " You must know the Commission is $600,000 in debt. But don't be uneasy. I've given my personal note for it." (he's worth more than that.) The next day he brought in the Belgian Minister of Finance who brought him $1,000,000 from the run-a-way Belgian Government. Both the English and the Belgian cabinets send for him about Belgian matters. He's a simple, modest, energetic little man who began his career in California; and he doesn't
and will end it in Heaven
want anybody's thanks. The surplus food being near Exhaustion in the U.S. & Canada, he has now begun on the Argentine, where the crop is just coming on. I introduced him to the Argentine Minister the other day, & the Minister said to me afterwards: " Somehow I feel like doing what that man asked me to do." A stone would weep to hear what Hoover has seen in Belgium — pitiful

U.S. Food Administrator

In 1917 after the United States entered the war, Hoover was called home by President Woodrow Wilson to become U.S. Food Administrator. Food from the U.S. was critical to the war effort, because one American ship could supply more food to Europe than two ships from South America or four from Australia. However, available ships were few, and enemy submarines blockading England and France were sinking more every day.

Mr. Hoover appealed to the American housewife to conserve food and eliminate waste. This helped reduce domestic consumption of food by 15 per cent, without government rationing. By promising a "fair price" for agricultural produce and guaranteeing markets for surplus, Hoover gained the cooperation of American farmers. The result was U.S. food shipments to Europe tripled. Hoovers program kept American armies fed and built up surplus stores of food to prevent a post-war famine in Europe. When the war ended suddenly, in November 1918, several Allied countries attempted to cancel their food orders to buy cheaper meat from other sources. Hoover kept his promise by stopping credit to those countries until they agreed to purchase the food surplus produced by American farmers in 1918.

American Relief Administration

Following the Armistice, President Wilson sent Hoover back to Europe as Director of the American Relief Administration. For eight months until the 1919 harvest the American Relief Administration was a major source of food for 300 million people in 21 countries in Europe and the Middle East. To fund this charitable work, President Wilson secured from congress a special appropriation of $100 million, but Senator Henry Cabot Lodge added

FOOD WILL WIN THE WAR
You came here seeking Freedom
You must now help to preserve it
WHEAT is needed for the allies
Waste nothing

an amendment which prohibited use of this money to feed any enemy countries. Germany was beaten, exhausted, and hungry. To force Germany to accept the allied peace terms, England and France maintained a food blockade of Germany.

Despite almost daily protests by Hoover at the Paris Peace Conference, the blockade continued. By mid-March the threat of famine in Germany was very real. Hoover diverted food cargoes intended for other parts into German harbors. The Allies protested, but President Wilson supported Hoover, and the blockade was cracked. To those who protested American feeding of Germany, Hoover replied:

". . . we do not kick a man in the stomach after we have licked him.

". . . we have not been fighting women and children, and we are not beginning now.

Before the blockade was officially lifted in late April, the German people received more than 75,000 tons of Food Administration stores, plus several thousand tons of C.R.B. foodstuff. Thousands were saved from starvation. Twenty years later the people of Germany remembered what Hoover had done for them. (See WWII Food Relief).

Left: "President Wilson's 'war cabinet.' Hoover is at top left."

Above: "Hoover's Message, by G. V. Millet (about 1918)."

HELPING HOOVER IN OUR
U.S. SCHOOL GARDEN

A.R.A. — European Children's Fund

Food distribution by the American Relief Administration officially ended on June 30, 1919. Soon afterwards, it became evident that children would suffer most from food shortages certain to develop during the next year. To combat this problem, Mr. Hoover created the A.R.A. — European Children's Fund. This private, charitable organization continued child-feeding in many areas of Europe through the summer of 1921. The focal point of the program was a hot lunch served in the schools, an idea which originated during the Belgian Relief in 1915. The European Children's Fund was supported by American donations and by the sale of FOOD DRAFT packages. This was the Origin of the CARE package.

Below: "A watercolor from children in Austria in thanks for the Hoover feeding programs. The Hoover Library collection includes hundreds of such tributes."

AMERICAN RELIEF ADMINISTRATION
Herbert Hoover, Chairman
Principles of Policy

1. *American personnel shall direct and supervise the handling and distribution of the relief in Europe.*
2. *The beneficiary of this relief shall understand that it is a gift of the American people, and that the identity of its origin must be preserved.*
3. *Relief must be confined to averting actual starvation, the ARA not being concerned in the alleviation of poverty per se.*
4. *Distribution must be made without regard to politics, race, religious creed, or social status.*
5. *American charity shall be withdrawn instantly whenever the economic recovery either of the nation or of a given locality enabled it to purchase outside supplies or whenever local supplies became sufficient to carry the population.*

THE MEN OF THE A.R.A.

"I still glow with pride at their reception in the countries where they worked. Many of these Americans serving abroad were officers and doughboys drawn from the American Army and Navy after the Armistice, men who in their civil life had not dealt with these or governmental problems, yet they showed such character and understanding that they won respect and personal affection wherever they went. Never was there such an exhibit of the power of the American way of life as these men presented, and they got a kick out of it — despite the surrounding tragedies. The misfits were so scarce that no one can recall their names.

Herbert Hoover
An American Epic, Vol. III

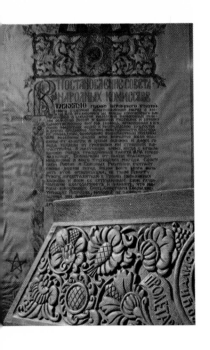

A.R.A. — Russian Famine

Russia was offered food relief in 1919, but refused to accept the terms of the A.R.A., which required that an American be in charge of all food stations to make certain food was not distributed on a political or religious basis. When Famine struck Russia in 1921, the Soviet government appealed to the world for help. Herbert Hoover immediately offered the assistance of the A.R.A., which was winding up its program of child-relief in Europe.

The U.S.S.R. finally accepted the terms of the A.R.A. and Hoover also stipulated that ALL AMERICAN PRISONERS be released. Although the State Department had a record of less than 20, more than 100 prisoners were released.

The A.R.A. fed Russia until the harvest of 1923. At the height of the famine, America was feeding 18 million Russian people.

RUSSIAN SCROLL

On July 10, 1923, the Council of Peoples Commissars of the Soviet Union presented a resolution of thanks to Herbert Hoover as Chairman of the American Relief Administration in gratitude for the aid the Russian people received from the United States during the 1921-1923 Russian famine. The resolution was hand-printed on a scroll of parchment mounted on embroidered silk, and enclosed in a handsomely carved chest.

Above: "ARA Feeding Station," by Vladimiroff (1922).

RESOLUTION OF THE SOVIET OF PEOPLES COMMISSARS

In the trying hour of a great and overwhelming disaster, the people of the United States, represented by the A.R.A., responded to the needs of the population, already exhausted by intervention and blockade, in the famine stricken parts of Russia and Federated Republics.

Unselfishly, the A.R.A. came to the aid of the people and organized on a broad scale the supply and distribution of food products and other articles of prime necessity.

Due to the enormous and entirely disinterested efforts of the A.R.A., millions of people of all ages were saved from death, and entire districts and even cities were saved from the horrible catastrophe which threatened them.

Now when the famine is over and the colossal work of the A.R.A. comes to a close, the Soviet of Peoples Commissars, in the name of the millions of people saved and in the name of all the working people of Soviet Russia and the Federated Republics counts it a duty to express before the whole world its deepest thanks to this organization, to its leader, Herbert Hoover, to its representative in Russia, Colonel Haskell, and to all its workers, and to declare that the people inhabiting the Union of Soviet Socialist Republics will never forget the help given them by the American people, through the A.R.A., seeing in it a pledge of the future friendship of the two nations.*

L. KAMENEV,
Acting President of the Council of Peoples Commissars.

N. GORBUNOV,
Chief of the Administrative Dept. of the Council of Peoples Commissars.

L. FOTIEVA,
Secretary of the Council of Peoples Commissars.
Moscow, Kremlin,
July 10, 1923.

Second Industrial Conference

In the immediate post-war era the United States economy was wracked by a series of strikes as organized labor sought to consolidate and expand its wartime gains. As the nation faced the prospects of simultaneous strikes in three basic industries — railroads, steel, and coal — President Wilson called an industrial conference composed of three groups representing labor, business, and the general public, but this conference quickly collapsed in a dispute over collective bargaining.

On November 16, 1919, President Wilson called a second industrial conference composed of leading men representing a cross section of the public interest. In the opening session of the conference Mr. Hoover was elected vice-chairman. Because the chairman attended only the opening and closing sessions, Mr. Hoover, in effect, was the chairman of the conference.

At the conclusion of its 86 meetings, the Industrial Conference issued a final report that contained a series of progressive recommendations designed to reduce industrial unrest:

1. Machinery for the voluntary settlement of industrial disputes
2. Employee representatives and recognition of the principle of collective bargaining
3. Cooperative system of food marketing
4. Establishment of minimum wages
5. Government studies of health, old age insurance and the cost of living
6. System of "gain sharing" as opposed to profit sharing
7. Prevention of child labor
8. Compulsory education and improved health programs
9. Equal pay for equal work for women
10. Better housing

Unfortunately these ideas were to far ahead of their time, and they were not accepted. Shortly after this report was issued, Mr. Hoover made an address before the Boston Chamber of Commerce on behalf of these proposals. He wrote in his *Memoirs* that "when I sat down from this address, the applause would not have awakened a nervous baby."

"President Woodrow Wilson."

Secretary
of Commerce
1921-1928

Secretary of Commerce (1921-1928)

When Herbert Hoover became Secretary of Commerce, efficiency, standardization, and elimination of waste became the guiding principles of a re-vitalized department. The over-all objective was to transform the department into a service agency which would benefit all the American people.

In addition to his governmental duties, he served actively as president of the American Child Health Association, Better Homes in America, and the American Engineering Council.

Before he left his cabinet position in 1928, it was said that Herbert Hoover was Secretary of Commerce and Under-Secretary of every other department in the Cabinet.

"Hoover and
President Calvin Coolidge, 1926."

Foreign and Domestic Commerce

The Bureau of Foreign and Domestic Commerce was completely overhauled, and two major objectives were established. The first was to make American business competitive with European exporters. The second was to break the European monopolies on strategic materials such as rubber and oil.

A new breed of commercial attaches was recruited. These men-knowledgeable in economics — were stationed over the world in strategic areas. Daily, weekly, and monthly reports poured into the Commerce Department, providing information on raw materials, domestic produce, laws, tariffs, duties, customs, climate, shipping services, and any other economic data that might be useful. This information was analyzed, organized, and immediately made available to the American commercial world. For the first time in history, the American businessman could compete on the world markets with the European exporter.

The British monopoly on world oil supplies was broken and raw rubber sources were developed in South America, the Philippine Islands, and Africa. Experimentation in synthetic rubber was given every assistance and encouragement. Six weeks after Pearl Harbor, Japan controlled the entire raw rubber supplies of the East Indies, which was then supplying most of the world's rubber.

Radio

Television

Bureau of Fisheries

Herbert Hoover established the principle that the airwaves were public property. In 1922 he called a National Radio Conference to solve a problem which suddenly developed in the broadcasting industry.

In 1921 there were two radio broadcasting stations. A year later more than 300 stations were fighting over the wave lengths to serve more than 600,000 radio receiving sets in the United States. At the Conference, Hoover proposed radio frequencies for the Army, Navy, Fire departments, Police departments, Commercial radio stations, and amateur "ham" radio stations. Accepting Hoover's allocation of wave lengths, the radio industry voluntarily regulated itself until federal legislation was enacted in 1927.

On April 7, 1927, Hoover participated in the first demonstration of television. The features and voice of Hoover in Washington, D.C., were transmitted by three telephone wires to American Telephone and Telegraph officials in New York City — one telephone line for the television current, one for his voice, and one line for synchronizing the sending and receiving motors. The voice heard through the telephone and the image on the small television screen synchronized perfectly in New York.

Left: "Hoover often used the radio to address the nation. The microphone he used for Station WRC in Washington, D.C., was presented to him in 1949."

The American fishing industry was declining rapidly when Hoover became Secretary of Commerce. Most endangered was the Alaskan Salmon. Illegal fishing methods were wide-spread, and several streams were fished out and dead. Hoover instituted strict measures to eliminate fish pirates and to protect spawning grounds. A treaty with Canada set up joint control of halibut and herring harvests in the North Pacific. Voluntary regulation in the Chesapeake saved the crab industry there. Other treaties and self-imposed limitations between rival companies curtailed abuses in other offshore fishing grounds.

Utilizing the press and civilian conservation organizations, Hoover successfully promoted a wide scale program of conservation, fish hatcheries, and re-stocking of lakes and streams.

A campaign against pollution of streams, harbors, and beaches began in 1921, and brought about Federal legislation in 1924 against pollution by oil-carrying ships.

Aviation

Hoover looked upon aviation as the transport of the future, and believed a strong commercial service was essential as a basis for national defense. He called the first Aviation Conference in 1922, inviting manufacturers, experienced pilots, and engineers to help draft the legislation which eventually established the Aeronautics Branch in the Department of Commerce.

The new service set out to make flying less colorful and more responsible. Engines and plane structures became subject to rigid examinations before they could be sold. Pilot training programs and testing were required before commercial licenses could be issued. Airports with landing lights, radio beacons, and weather information were developed in major cities. Emergency landing fields became commonplace between major airports and ground-to-air radio communications were developed.

In its first three years, the new Aeronautics Branch promoted construction of more than 1,200 airports and 25,000 miles of government improved airways. By 1928 America was leading the world in aircraft production, with the lowest accident rate for miles traveled.

Above: "Hoover and aviator Charles Lindbergh, 1927."

Street and Highway Safety

In 1923 more than 20,000 Americans died in auto accidents, another 600,000 were injured, and property damage exceeded $600 million. When these figures became public, Hoover called a National Conference on Street and Highway Safety in Washington. Out of the conference came a model vehicle code, covering driver's licenses, auto registration, and standardized highway traffic laws. To dramatize the need for uniform traffic laws and a motor vehicle code, two autos were sent across country in opposite directions. The west-bound car followed New York traffic laws. The east-bound car obeyed the traffic laws of San Francisco. One car received 18 traffic citations, while the other received 22 citations.

The uniform code of traffic regulations was adopted, with minor variations, by every state and most municipalities. While the new code did not bring an end to traffic fatalities, the number of deaths per 100 cars on the road was reduced significantly.

Standardization and Better Homes

Hoover's policy of elimination of waste brought standardization and simplification into every home in America. Threads on nuts, bolts and screws were standardized. Auto wheels and tires were reduced from eight to three standard sizes. Milk bottles were reduced from 49 to four standard sizes , bed springs from 78 sizes to four, and bricks from 44 to one.

In addition, standardization regulated weighing and measuring devices and public utility meters, such as gas, water, and taxi.

"The only case where unlimited diversification seems justified is padlock keys," Hoover commented at the time.

Standardization revolutionized the building industry. Standard cuts of lumber, and sizes of brick, modular construction and standardized plumbing and electrical fixtures produced better homes at lower cost. The Housing Division of the Bureau of Standards developed additives for concrete which made winter construction possible, and increased employment in the industry.

Better Homes In America, founded by Hoover, made available to the public the new ideas and improvements devloped by the Housing Division. It was the first "do-it-yourself" program organized for the benefit of the average home owner.

Child Health

Herbert Hoover served as President of the American Child Health Association for 15 years, and raised funds annually from private sources to finance health education in the schools and promotion of child health programs on the community level. Early in the history of the Association he formulated the Child's Bill of Rights, which has been called the *Magna Carta of Childhood.*

Through health education in schools and community organizations, children and parents were educated on the basic elements of good health. Child hygiene departments or bureaus were created in 47 states and in hundreds of cities. Immunization and vaccination against diptheria and small pox practically eliminated the two major scourges of infancy and childhood.

Supplementary milk and hot lunch programs were supported in areas where undernourishment in children was evident.

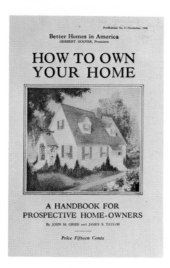

THE CHILD'S BILL OF RIGHTS

*T*he ideal to which we should strive is that there shall be no child in America:

That has not been born under proper conditions.

That does not live in hygienic surroundings.

That ever suffers from undernourishment.

That does not have prompt and efficient medical attention and inspection.

That does not receive primary instruction in the elements of hygiene and good health.

That has not the complete birthright of a sound mind in a sound body.

That has not the encouragement to express in fullest measure the spirit within, which is the final endowment of every human being.

Herbert Hoover.

Miss Spinach, with her gown of green
And juicy Mr. Pea,
With Lettuce's green ruffles,
As fresh as fresh can be,
And tall, thin Mr. Celery,
And Cabbage and String Bean,
All make us feel like singing,
"The eating of the green!"

Hoover Dam

For many years the lower Colorado River Valley experienced devastation from spring floods and summer droughts. Many futile attempts had been made to harness the river. The only logical solution was a high dam which could control the waters during the flood stage and release it during the dry season.

In 1921 Hoover became Chairman of the Colorado River Commission. He presided at meetings of the Commission which culminated in the formation of the Colorado River Compact,

between the states affected. For seven years he campaigned for ratification of the Compact by state legislatures.

Construction was authorized and work began in 1930. The dam was completed and dedicated in 1936 as "Boulder Dam." On April 30, 1947, President Truman signed the bill which restored the name "Hoover Dam."

Mississippi Flood — 1927

The disastrous Mississippi Flood in 1927 drove more than a million people from their homes. Under Mr. Hoover's direction, tent cities were erected on high ground near the flooded areas. In these camps, many children received a balance diet for the first time in their lives and many more received their first vaccinations and other medical treatment. Through appeals by radio and the press, Mr. Hoover headed a drive which raised $15 million for the Red Cross. He obtained a grant of $1 million from the Rockefeller Foundation for post-flood sanitation. Through the U.S. Chamber of Commerce he created the Flood-Credits Corporation which made available $10 million in low-interest loans to small farmers and businessmen. No federal funds were involved in this $26 million operation.

The Presidency
1929 - 1933

Inauguration/ Election 1928-1929

Herbert Hoover was inaugurated as 31st President on March 4, 1929. (The inaugural date was changed to January 20 during Franklin Roosevelt's term.) Hoover's candidacy had been sought by both major parties, and as early as 1920 he had won Democratic primaries for the presidential nomination in several states. With him on the Republican ticket in 1928 was Charles Curtis, Senator from Kansas.

Hoover campaigned on a program advocating construction and progress, but one which reminded voters that:

"The points of contact between the government and the people are constantly multiplying. Every year wise governmental policies become more vital in ordinary life. As our problems grow, so do our temptations grow to venture away from those principles upon which our republic was founded and upon which it has grown to greatness."

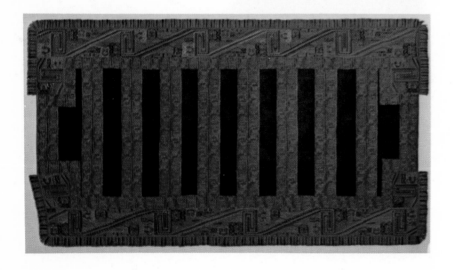

South American Tour — 1928

Shortly after his election in 1928, Hoover made a six week tour of Latin America. As Secretary of Commerce he had been disturbed by the "Colossus of the North" attitude prevalent in U.S. foreign policy toward Latin America. His trip to ten latin American countries stressed the theme of "the good neighbor." The results of that trip were positive: withdrawal of American troops from Latin America and the establishment of inter'American aviation.

PARACUS MANTLE
Among the gifts Hoover received during his South American tour was the 2000 year old Paracus Mantle from Peru. The mantle had been discovered at a burial site of the pre-Incan Paracus Culture of southern Peru. Protection at the burial site from air, moisture, and light had preserved the alpaca wool robe through the centuries. The mantle was restored in 1957 by the American Museum of Natural History, a process which took six months and included cleaning, blocking, replacement of missing fringe, and mounting.

Goals as President

Hoover entered the office of the Presidency determined to maintain the integrity of the executive branch and to respect the independence of the legislative branch. He chose cabinet members who were successful administrators and men of public esteem.

He set himself three major tasks as President: continuation of the development programs he had begun as Secretary of Commerce; reforms in social and business life; and reorientation of U.S. foreign policy toward cooperation for peace and international progress. The methods used to achieve these goals would be ones which would preserve personal liberty. However, he had hardly begun on these programs when the stock market crash and the economic consequence of World War I exploded into alarming economic conditions for the world.

Above: "President Hoover and Vice-President Charles Curtis."

PRESIDENT HOOVER'S
CABINET

SECRETARY OF STATE
  Frank B. Kellogg, Henry L.
  Stimson (1929)
SECRETARY OF TREASURY
  Andrew W. Mellon, Ogden L.
  Mills (1932)
SECRETARY OF WAR
  James W. Good, Patrick J.
  Hurley (1929)

SECRETARY OF NAVY
  Charles F. Adams
ATTORNEY GENERAL
  William D. Mitchell
SECRETARY OF
  AGRICULTURE
  Arthur M. Hyde
SECRETARY OF COMMERCE
  Robert P. Lamont, Roy D.
  Chapin (1932)
SECRETARY OF INTERIOR
  Ray Layman Wilbur
SECRETARY OF LABOR
  James J. Davis, William N.
  Doak (1930)
POSTMASTER GENERAL
  Walter F. Brown

Child Health Conference

Hoover continued the programs he had begun on child welfare and better housing during the commerce years. In 1930 the first White House Conference on Child Health was called, assembling 1200 delegates from across the country. The conference stimulated state and municipal action for the protection of children by instituting health programs in schools, improving local health ordinances, promoting nursery schools and kindergartens, plus instituting programs to train parents in child care.

Conservation of Natural Resources

Concerned with conservation of natural resources, Hoover checked abuses of private oil permits on public land, increased acreage of national forests by 2,250,000 acres, expanded 16 national parks and created nine new areas, and made recommendations for the conservation of fisheries, minerals, and grazing lands.

"Skyline Drive, Shenandoah National Park."

Inland Waterways

As President, Hoover advocated the development of water resources. The Colorado River Compact, of which Hoover had been the architect as Secretary of Commerce, was approved and work started on the giant dam. The Bureau of Reclamation also completed the engineering for Grand Coulee Dam and planned a system of dams for the central valley of California and the Tennessee River. The important River and Harbors Bill of 1930 provided for an inland waterway system. Flood control was completed on the lower Mississippi, the canal system expanded in the East, and the Great Lakes — St. Lawrence Waterway Treaty signed with Canada. The treaty, however, was not approved by Congress until 1953.

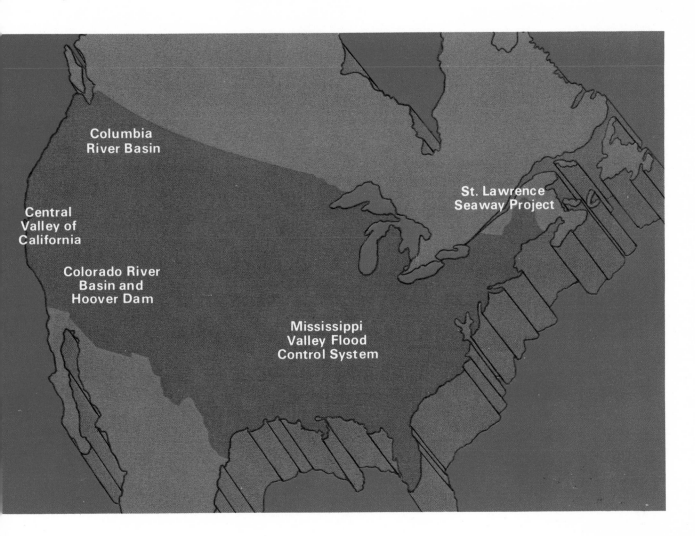

Public Works

Other Presidential programs included needed public works. The San Francisco Bay Bridge was begun, highway construction added 37,000 miles to the nation's highways, and in Washington, D.C., a new system of parks and federal buildings helped beautify the city.

Above: "Hoover lays the cornerstone for the new Department of Commerce building."

Aviation

During President Hoover's term, a system of commercial airways was established, service improved, and air mail costs reduced. His 1928 tour of Central and South America had laid the foundations for Latin American air service. In March, 1930 mail contracts were announced to Central America, Columbia, Ecuador, and Peru. In October 1930, Argentina, Brazil, and Uruguay were added to the service.

Above: "President Hoover and aviatrix Amelia Earhart."

Reform — Social

In addition to his involvement with child care and better housing, Hoover's interest in social reform included proposals for instituting old age assistance and unemployment compensation. The progress of these programs, however, was halted by the burdens of the depression. Hoover's childhood summer on the Osage Reservation had also concerned him with the problems of the Indian. He appointed two respected Quakers to administer the Indian Bureau with the objective to help the Indians become self-supporting and self-respecting.

Reform — Executive

Ever mindful of the integrity of the Presidential office, Hoover began his reforms with the executive branch. Attacking the patronage system, he increased the number of federal employees covered by the merit system of the Civil Service Act. He fought for more efficient organization of the executive departments, but Congress blocked his proposals. Hoover later implemented proposals with the Hoover Commissions under Presidents Truman and Eisenhower.

Reform — Law

In law reform he raised the standards for judicial officials and enacted reforms in procedure for criminal cases. He also proposed reforms in bankruptcy laws and signed a series of prison reform acts which included the establishment of separate facilities for juveniles and lesser offenders. Prohibition was a more difficult area. Hoover believed that as President he had a duty to enforce the laws. As the states had delegated more and more enforcement to the federal government, Hoover found it necessary to expand federal enforcement agencies. His enforcement of prohibition was moderately successful. The conviction of Chicago gangster Al Capone was accomplished during his term.

Foreign Affairs and National Defense

In the area of foreign policy, President Hoover's ambition was to lead the U.S. in full cooperation with world moral forces to preserve peace.

To improve relations with Latin America, the President put into practice the Good Neighbor Policy he had announced on his 1928 trip. Troops were withdrawn from Nicaragua and Haiti. Regular air communications were established with several South American countries. The President publicly stated that the United States would not become involved in the domestic affairs of other American Republics.

The Foreign Service was reorganized and political appointees were removed as ambassadors and ministers. They were replaced with career men or otherwise independent persons who had a background and familiarity with the people, the language, and the customs of the country.

The President's policies on national defense and world disarmament had a simple objective. That was to insure freedom from war to the American people. To this end, the country's

military and naval forces were improved and stablized at a level which would discourage any aggressor who might have designs on the Western Hemisphere.

While the United States was not a member of the League of Nations, it did join in several treaties promoting control of narcotics, international regulation of radio, and protection of intellectual properties by international copyright. Treaties of arbitration were signed with 25 nations, and treaties of conciliation were signed with 17.

"Hoover at the Palace in Santiago, Chili, 1928."

Disarmament and Moral Forces for Peace

National defense policies and needs were determined by the armaments of those who might threaten American security. To reduce this threat, President Hoover proposed in 1929 a Naval Disarmament Conference to discuss limitation of warships. To set the stage for the conference, the President invited British Prime Minister Ramsey MacDonald to Washington for preliminary discussions. The two men spent several days at Hoover's Rapidan Camp, where they layed the groundwork for a Naval Conference in London the following year. The Naval Limitation Treaty, resulting from the London Conference, was ratified by the Senate on July 22, 1930.

In 1931, the entire world was shocked by the Japanese invasion of Manchuria. While it was an act of aggression and a violation of the Nine-Power Treaty of 1922,

Right: "Hoover and Prime Minister Mac-Donald held secluded talks at the President's hideaway at Camp Rapidan."

President Hoover resisted all attempts by those advocating economic sanctions or other pressures which might lead to hostilities with Japan. The United States was prepared to defend the Western Hemisphere, but it was not capable of sustaining a war 8,000 miles across the ocean. Hoover was also aware that the U.S. could not be assured of aid from another major power in such a conflict.

Accordingly, he adopted the strongest moral position possible short of actual conflict, the

promotion of the "non-recognition" policy. Aside from military defense of the Western Hemisphere, Hoover believed that America had two alternatives in foreign policy. The first was moral standards of conduct, supported with moral forces. The second was economic and inevitably military force against aggression. Hoover chose the first alternative. It was not isolationism; it was the long range belief that there must somehow be an abiding place for law and a sanctuary for civilization.

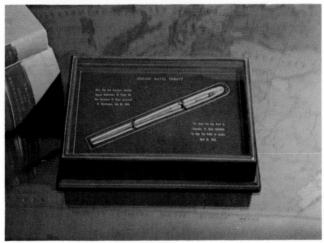

Living in the White House

Living in the White House, Herbert Hoover wrote, was living with the invisible presence of the leaders of our country. It was a house of tradition. Too many traditions, Hoover thought. One of the traditions gradually banished was the numerous receptions at which anyone could come to shake the President's hand. He felt the President spent too much time seeing people and not enough time in serious work. His was a busy day, begun each morning with a medicine ball game on the White House lawn at 7:30 a.m.

Mrs. Hoover served as a gracious White House hostess, taking great care to see to the comfort of all guests. She made a careful study of White House furnishings and assembled a notebook filled with photographs, descriptions and history. As First Lady she was named honorary president of the Girls Scouts and actively worked to increase the membership and resources of the organization. Her sons grown, she planned special events for staff children or visiting grandchildren, and donated time and money to many charities. Newspaper reporters sent to interview the First Lady commented on her dignity, sincerity, and ability to put a person at ease.

Because of the extreme summer heat of Washington in the days before air-conditioning, the President looked for a country retreat. President Hoover chose an isolated location in the Blue Ridge Mountains of Virginia. Calling it Camp Rapidan, he ordered the

construction of log cabins and retreated to the camp for fishing and relaxation. He personally paid for all building and upkeep and at the end of his term donated the land to the newly-created Shenandoah National Park.

Two important, but widely differing events occurred at the White House during the Hoover term. One was the White House fire of 1929 and the other the visit of the King and Queen of Siam in 1931. Fire broke out in the west wing of the White House on Christmas Eve while the Hoovers were entertaining staff children at a party. The men, including the President, quietly left to see to the situation while the party continued. The fire burned from the basement to the roof and

gutted Hoover's office. He moved to the Navy Building until the office could be restored.

The visit of the King and Queen was the first official visit of an absolute monarch to the White House. The royal couple visited Washington officially for three days and were entertained at a State Dinner.

"A 1930 Christmas gift from Mrs. Hoover to one of the children present on the night of the White House fire."

Left: "Enameled miniature in a circle of diamonds of the King of Siam."

Fight Against Speculation

When Hoover took office in March, 1929, America was riding a wave of prosperity. Much of it was false prosperity, however, based on speculative values and supported by the easy credit policies of the Federal Reserve Board. These policies made it easy for anyone to borrow money for speculation.

Both before and after his innauguration, Hoover attempted to ease the pressure before the inevitable explosion, but the speculation fever had gone too far. The Reserve Board policies were reversed, but the public continued to borrow. Through editors of major newspapers Hoover warned against the dangers of speculation, but the public ignored strong editorials. He pleaded with bankers to curb market speculation, but they scoffed and declared the market sound. He urged the President of the New York exchange to curb manipulation of stock. Promises were made, but no action resulted. In October, 1929, the market collapsed.

Immediately following the crash, Hoover called leaders of business, industry, and labor to the White House where agreements were reached and carried out to preserve employment and wages, to share the work, and to prevent strikes and lockouts. With the cooperation of state governors and mayors of major cities, the President launched the greatest program of federal, state, and local public works program in history up to that date. Construction expenditures reached $6 billion in 1929 and $7 billion in 1930. William Green, President of the AFL commented in October, 1930:

"As we emerge from this distressing period of unemployment we are permitted to understand and appreciate the value of the service which the President rendered the wage earners of the country and industry when he convened the White House conferences to which I have just referred."

Below: "President Hoover with Walter Gifford, chairman of the President's Committee for Unemployment Relief."

Below: "President Hoover leaving the Senate after an address requesting authorization for the RFC to lend money to the states for relief, May, 1932."

Unemployment Agriculture Relief

In September, 1930, Hoover initiated the Presidents Committee on Unemployment Relief, to care for those in distress during the winter of 1930-31. A national committee and 3,000 state, county and local committees were established to see that no one suffered from cold or hunger during the winter months. By October they were functioning, and reported to the President that all needs could be met. When local committees were overtaxed, they were aided by state committees, and these in turn by the national committee. Pressure from radical groups for direct federal doles were resisted when local and state committees and the Red Cross emphatically declared they were meeting all needs brought to their attention. In fact, they were searching out needy families who were resisting charity out of pride.

The President held ready federal aid to any state with distress beyond its means, but he insisted that any federal aid granted to a state would be distributed by a non-partisan committee. Hoover feared direct federal aid because it would "destroy local responsibility," and because it would "bring a train of corruption and waste such as our nation had never witnessed."

The Committee continued to operate through the depression, and no state committee asked for federal aid. The clerical expenses for the national committee, in 1932, were raised from private sources, part of them from the President's "own pocket."

The Federal Farm Board was created by a special session of Congress called by Hoover in April, 1929. With a capital of $500 million, its aim was to build up farmers cooperatives and decrease destructive competition, while holding a floor under farm prices. The Board was barely underway when the crash occured, so it became an emergency depression remedy. It saved thousands of farmers by cushioning the drastic price drops in the 1929 and 1930

marketing season, and prevented panic in the agricultural markets.

A calamity hit agriculture in 1930, when the Midwest and South experienced the worst drought since 1881. A million farm families were destitute and 20,000,000 farm animals were threatened with destruction. The President secured reduced rates on feedstuffs shipped into the needy areas, and expanded Federal construction to supplement income. State drought relief committees were established, and the Red Cross set aside $5 million for relief. In January the President led a public appeal which raised another $5 million. Federal seed loans supplemented state loans, and public appeals brought more than 600 carloads of food into the stricken areas — donated by Northern, Eastern, and Pacific States, and delivered free of charge by the railroads.

In spite of the drought, bumper grain crops were harvested in other areas, further depressing farm prices. The Farm Board lost $100 million holding a floor under the market, but saved many times that amount for the farmers.

Left: "The Red cross provided relief assistance for victims of the 1930 drought."

Left: "President Hoover signing bill creating Federal Farm Board, 1929."

Financial Collapse of Europe, 1931

The economic consequences of the Peace of Versailles began to surface in Europe early in 1931. World War I had weakened the economic structure of every nation in Europe, especially Germany and Austria. Stripped of their wealth and saddled with reparations, they were living on short-term credit, borrowing today to pay off the loans due tomorrow. In March, 1931, when they formed a customs union, French banks called in their short-term loans. Austria's largest bank failed, followed by failures in Germany, Hungary, and others in central Europe. American exports ceased abruptly, and European banks began dumping American securities on the market. Gold and short-term credit rolled from country to country like a bowling ball on the deck of a ship.

After weeks of negotiations, Hoover obtained an international moratorium of one year on all reparations and war debts. Farm prices rose, for a short period. Hoover then negotiated a "standstill" agreement, whereby private commercial loans to central European countries would be frozen until February, 1932.

French bankers balked, but finall[y] participated. In September, French gold was withdrawn from English banking houses and the Bank of England defaulted on gol[d] payments. Denmark, Sweden, Norway and Holland followed. Gold runs began on U.S. banks. American exports came to a halt, and farm prices hit bottom.

WHERE THE MOST OF IT GOES

Banking Reform

The European financial collapse and drain of U.S. gold caused havoc in the banking world. A banking reform act, advocated by Hoover since 1929, was still in committee and bank failures were increasing. In October, 1931, Hoover called a series of conferences in Washington, resulting in the National Credit Association with a bank credit pool of $5 million. The crisis eased and failures decreased, but only for a short time. The Credit Association became ultra-conservative and fearful, and later disbanded.

When business leaders gave up and asked the government to do their job, Hoover created the RFC and Home Loan Banks. The Bank Credit Act, signed by Hoover in February, 1932, eased the drain on gold. The RFC Home Loan Banks, and Farm Board support of Land Banks diminished failures and foreclosures of homes and farms.

In the summer of 1932, the situation improved, but again optimism was short-lived. With the elections in November, business activity came to a halt, waiting for an indication of monetary policies by the new administration.

On January 4, 1933, a House resolution forced publication of the names of banks that had borrowed from the RFC. There was an immediate run on the banks, and by the end of the month 62 of them had closed their doors. Despite protests by the RFC Board, Hoover, Senator Carter Glass, and other congressional leaders, the disclosures continued.

Until he stepped down from office on March 4, President Hoover never stopped working to stem the banking panic. His last phone call on the crisis was made at 11 p.m., March 3, 1933.

The new antitoxin.

Analysis

When the depression began in the autumn of 1929, President Hoover initiated a policy unprecedented in American history. He was the first President to commit the full power and resources of the government to fight a depression. He was the first President to use his office as a rallying force to stir private enterprise into a cooperative effort to help themselves and to help their neighbors in time of distress.

Hoover originated the greatest private program ever created in this country for direct relief of distress. Through personal effort and sacrifice he kept it functioning in the face of opposition from those who would abandon their own responsibilities and pass the burden on to the Federal Government. He warned the American people they must take care of their own neighbors in time of distress. He warned them that if they passed this responsibility on to the Federal Government, they would be creating a monster that eventually could destroy their country.

Herbert Hoover was the only one, unfortunately, who recognized a dangerous fork in the road before it was passed. He feared that bureaucratic statism would create an inevitable train of corruption and waste such as the country had never witnessed before. He feared that federal aid — if not handled very carefully — would devalue the human beings it claimed to save. He feared that once direct federal aid began, it would get out of control.

In 1933 Mayor Smith and Banker Jones were asking the Federal Government to assume responsibility for feeding their hungry neighbors. In 1973 the children of Mayor Smith and Banker Jones were asking the Federal Government to assume responsibility for building sidewalks around the local courthouse .

The Post-Presidential Years

Interlude

In March, 1933, the Hoovers returned to their home on the Stanford campus. Here they could enjoy the pleasures for which there had been little time since that day in 1914 when Ambassador Page called Hoover for help in repatriating stranded Americans in London. Hoover went fishing, organized Boys' Clubs, and enjoyed his grandchildren, while Mrs. Hoover continued her work with the Girl Scouts. As they became more involved in charitable activities, they found it convenient to live part time in New York City, although they retained their home at Stanford.

On January 7, 1944, Lou Henry Hoover died suddenly of a heart attack. A gracious woman, who spoke several languages and mastered housekeeping in many parts of the world, she was remembered for her dignity, sincerity and warmth. Following her wishes, their California home was given to Stanford University.

CALIFORNIA, HERE I COME

MAR 5 1933

HOOVER

Hoover Institution

In the early days of WWI, Hoover conceived the idea of an institution to promote peace by studying the causes of war and revolution. At his own expense he began collecting documents relating to the World War and the revolution in Russia, and shipped them to Stanford University. In 1941 the new research library, The Hoover Institution on War, Revolution, and Peace, was dedicated. Hoover Institution publication No. 108 was published in 1973, and many more studies are continuing.

Above: "Herbert Hoover with two of his grandchildren, Lou Henry Hoover and Allan Henry Hoover."

Boy's Club of America

Herbert Hoover served as Chairman of the Boys' Clubs of America for 28 years, establishing more than 500 new Boys' Clubs and raising over 100 million for construction of buildings. To Herbert Hoover, every American boy deserved an "equal opportunity" to grow into a moral, productive citizen. The Boys' Clubs help them achieve that goal.

WHAT IS A BOY?

"Together with his sister, the boy is our most precious possession. But he presents not only joys and hopes, but also paradoxes. He strains our nerves, yet he is a complex of cells, teeming with affection. He is a periodic nuisance yet he is a joy forever. He is a part-time incarnation of destruction; yet he radiates sunlight to all the world. He gives evidence of being the child of iniquity, yet he makes a great nation. He is filled with curiosity as to every mortal thing. He is an illuminated interrogation point, yet he is the most entertaining animal that is."
Herbert Hoover

HERBERT HOOVER BUILDING
NATIONAL HEADQUARTERS
BOYS CLUB OF AMERICA -N.Y.C-

BOYS' CLUBS GROWTH UNDER HERBERT HOOVER

	1936	1964
Named Board Chairman	10/19/36	
Board Membership	40	133
Number of Clubs	140	645 (Approx.)
Number of Boys' Club Cities	148	410
Number of Boys' Clubs States	34	46
Total Boy Membership	140,000	600,000 plus
National Budget	$85,000	$1,300,000
Total Budget for Boys' Clubs	$2,500,000	$20,000,000
Replacement Value of Buildings & Equipment	$20,000,000	$135,000,000
Growth Rate	5-10 Clubs per year	25-30 Clubs per year

Left: " the national headquarters of the Boys' Clubs in New York City, dedicated October 18, 1960, was named for Herbert Hoover."

Trip to Europe — 1938

In February, 1938, Hoover returned to Belgium to be honored by the men who had served with him during the WWI relief operations. The old Comité National, which had directed operations in Belgium, met again after 20 years. They all occupied their old seat while the Chairman called the roll.

"I have seldom been more affected than by that roll call, and the frequent reply, 'Mort.' More than one-third of the chairs were empty . . . We all had difficulty in completing our sentences."

World War II Food Relief 1939-1942

When Hitler and Stalin joined forces in 1939 and sent their armies into Poland and Finland, the call for food relief again reached Herbert Hoover. Rallying veterans of the ARA and CRB, he organized the Finnish Relief Fund and the Commission for Polish Relief. A year later, when Germany invaded Belgium, the Belgian Relief Fund was established. Later, the three funds were combined as the "Food for the Small Democracies."

When France fell in 1940, a shipping blockade cut off direct sea access to Poland and Belgium. Food for Belgium landed in Lisbon and was transported by German soldiers through France to Belgium. Other food was landed in Genoa and was transported by German soldiers into Poland. The soldiers did not touch one grain of "Hoover's Wheat." Twenty years before in 1919 Hoover had fed these same Germans when they were starving.

Hoover's WWII relief efforts continued until Pearl Harbor, December 7, 1941.

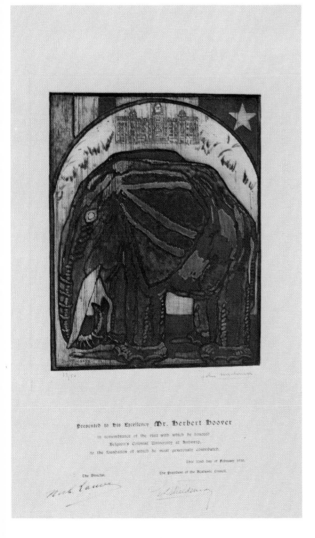

Return to Public Service 1945-46

In May, 1945, President Truman called Herbert Hoover back to Public Service, to advise on the feeding of hungry people in Europe. Mr. Hoover caught the first train for Washington.

Early in 1946, President Truman became uneasy about world food shortages. After a global war and a disasterous harvest in 1945, nations of Europe and Asia were faced with the greatest famine in History.

Again he called on Hoover, this time to make a world famine survey. Though he was 71 years of age, Hoover accepted the call. In less than three months he traveled 51,000 miles through 38 countries, pinpointing the worst famine regions and recommending to the President the areas where American food was needed most urgently. The combined efforts of these two American Presidents saved millions from death by starvation.

Hoover Commissions

The steady growth in the size of government has long disturbed Presidents, Congressmen, and American Statesmen. Repeated efforts have been made to slow it down and make it more efficient and manageable. In the late 19th century two committees attempted the task. In the early 20th century two more committees tried. In the 1920's and again in 1936-37 attempts were made to cut down the ever-increasing size of government. For the most part these efforts were ineffective, mainly because there was no public support.

The most serious and far reaching studies were the two commissions headed by Herbert Hoover, 1947-1949 under President Truman, and 1953-1955 under President Eisenhower. Many recommendations of the first Hoover Commission were implemented and great economies realized, only to be wiped out by the Korean War. The recommendations of the second Hoover Commission are largely dormant, again through lack of public support.

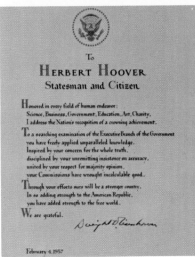

"Members of the first Hoover Commission. Seated: George Mead, Herbert Hoover, President Harry Truman, Joseph Kennedy, John L. McClellan. Standing: Clarence J. Brown, James Forrestal, Arthur S. Flemming, James H. Rowe, Jr., Dean Acheson, James K. Pollock, Carter Manasco. Not pictured: George D. Aiken.

Recognitions in the Autumn Years

WEST BERLIN 1954

In 1954 Mr. Hoover returned to Berlin as the personal guest of Chancellor Konrad Adenauer. He was honored as a humanitarian and statesman, with special recognition for his efforts to achieve more enlightened policies toward Germany during his post-war fact-finding tour for President Truman. He stated on Germany's recovery:

There can be no better evidence of that recovery than in the children. Eight years ago the deadpan of undernourishment shown in their faces. They were spiritless and but few were playing in the streets. This week hosts of healthy, chattering, vivacious and happy faces have turned out to greet me everywhere.

Herbert Hoover was a man to whom recognition came from all sectors. The engineer, the humanitarian, the public servant — all phases of his many-faceted career drew awards. He received over 175 medals, numerous plaques, citations, testimonials, honorary memberships and honorary citizenships. Streets, avenues, schools, and even an asteroid were named for him. But his most prized possessions remained those tributes from the children for whom he worked to ensure their future.

Herbert Hoover received a record number of honorary degrees, both American and foreign, from small college and large university. He accepted 45 honorary degrees from United States Universities and 21 honorary degrees from foreign universities, and was offered 19 more which he was unable to accept because his many obligations prevented his fulfilling the requirement of attendance. His first honorary degree was from Brown University in 1916; his last degree was awarded posthumously in 1965 from McKendree College in Illinois.

Left: "Hoover is presented a bouquet during a visit to a West German refugee camp."

Schools Named After Herbert Hoover

"No greater honor may come to an American," said Herbert Hoover concerning the use of his name on school buildings. Sixty-one schools, including one in West Berlin, West Germany, bear his name. As he said: "There is no part of our life with which I would rather be associated than the education of our young people, for within it lies the basis for our future."

CALIFORNIA
Burlingame
Fresno
Glendale
Indio
Lakewood
Long Beach
Los Angeles
Merced
Oakland
Palo Alto
Redwood City
San Diego
San Francisco
San Jose
Santa Ana
Stockton
Westminster

FLORIDA
Indialantic

ILLINOIS
Calumet City

IOWA
Bettendorf
Cedar Rapids
Council Bluffs
Davenport
Des Moines
Dubuque
Iowa City
Mason City
Sioux City
Toledo
Waterloo
West Branch

MARYLAND
Rockville

MASSACHUSETTS
Melrose

MICHIGAN
Flint
Hazel Park
Lincoln Park
Livonia

MINNESOTA
Anoka
Mankato
Rochester

NEW JERSEY
Bergenfield
Edison

NEW MEXICO
Albuquerque

NEW YORK
Kenmore

OKLAHOMA
Bartlesville
Enid
Lawton
Oklahoma City
Tulsa

OREGON
Corvallis
Medford
Salem

PENNSYLVANIA
Camp Hill
Harrisburg
Penndel
Pittsburgh

WEST VIRGINIA
Clendenin

WISCONSIN
Neenah
New Berlin

WASHINGTON
Yakima

"NO GREATER HONOR MAY COME TO AN AMERICAN THAN TO HAVE A SCHOOL NAMED AFTER HIM"

Last Public Duties

Mr. Hoover's last official duty was to serve as the special United States representative to the Brussels World's Fair in 1958. In his speech at the American pavilion on July 4, 1958, Mr. Hoover said:

Mine has been a long life. In that time I have lived and worked among more than 50 nations. I have not visited them as a tourist. I have had some part in the lives of their people.

In October, 1964, Herbert Hoover read a news item that an old friend had fallen, injuring himself. Although seriously ill at the time, he asked that the following telegram be sent to Harry Truman. This was Herbert Hoover's last communication. He died on October 20, 1964.

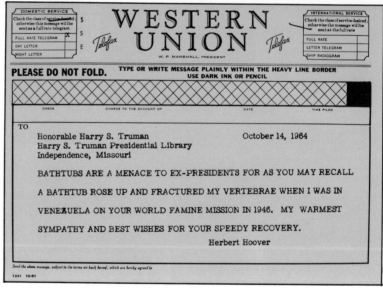

WESTERN UNION

PLEASE DO NOT FOLD.   TYPE OR WRITE MESSAGE PLAINLY WITHIN THE HEAVY LINE BORDER
USE DARK INK OR PENCIL

TO

Honorable Harry S. Truman   October 14, 1964
Harry S. Truman Presidential Library
Independence, Missouri

BATHTUBS ARE A MENACE TO EX-PRESIDENTS FOR AS YOU MAY RECALL

A BATHTUB ROSE UP AND FRACTURED MY VERTEBRAE WHEN I WAS IN

VENEZUELA ON YOUR WORLD FAMINE MISSION IN 1946. MY WARMEST

SYMPATHY AND BEST WISHES FOR YOUR SPEEDY RECOVERY.

                                    Herbert Hoover

Funeral

Herbert Hoover died in his suite at the Waldorf-Astoria on October 20, 1964, and his flag draped coffin was carried with full military honors to Washington, D.C., to lie in state in the Capitol Rotunda. On October 25, 80,000 people assembled in West Branch to observe the burial ceremony on a grassy knoll only a few hundred yards from the small cottage where the nation's 31st President was born.

From Herbert Hoover on His 90th Birthday

Our American form of civilization has been deluged with rising criticism, from both home and abroad. Altogether, the critics say, we seem to be in a very, very bad way, and engaged in our decline and fall.

Criticism is no doubt good for the soul, but we must beware that it does not upset our confidence in ourselves. So perhaps the time has come for Americans to take stock and to think something good about themselves.

We could point to our constantly improving physical health and lengthening span of life.

In the governmental field, we could suggest that our supposedly "decadent" people still rely upon the miracle of the ballot and the legislative hall to settle differences of view, and not upon a secret police.

In the cultural field, we could point out that we have more young people in high school and institutions of higher learning, more musical and literary organizations, greater distribution of the printed and spoken word than any other country.

On the moral and spiritual side, we could suggest that we alone, of all nations, fought for free men in two world wars and asked no indemnities, no acquisition of territory, no domination over other peoples. We could point to a spirit of Christian compassion such as the world has never seen, and prove it by the tons of food and clothing and billions of dollars we have provided as gifts in saving hundreds of millions of people overseas from famine and many governments from collapse.

Deeply as I feel the lag in certain areas which denies equal chance to our Negro population, I cannot refrain from saying that our 19 million Negroes probably own more automobiles than all the 220 million Russians and the 200 million African Negroes put together.

We have an alarming amount of crime and youth delinquency. The fault, however, has been largely in the failure of our law enforcement after the police have made the arrest.

Hope lies in the continuing expansion of such organizations as the Boys' Clubs of America that take underprivileged boys off the streets during their formative years and help them to build sound minds and sound bodies and, most important of all, sound characters.

We could point out that our American system has achieved the great productivity, the highest standard of living of any nation on earth. True, we have large natural resources — but other nations also have such resources. What, then, has brought us such abundance?

I have enjoyed a varied life and wide opportunities to discover the key. I have seen America in contrast with many nations and races. My profession took me into many foreign lands under many kinds of government. I have worked with their great spiritual leaders and their great statesmen. I have seen freedom die and slavery arise. I have worked in governments of free men, of tyrannies, of socialists and of communists.

I have searched in these travels — and have sought to learn from books and from the leaders of other nations — what it is that has given America this super-abundance. What is the key to it?

The key, I am convinced, is that among us there is greater freedom for the individual man and woman than in any other great nation. In the Constitution and in the Bill of Rights are enumerated the specific freedoms. Then there are a dozen other freedoms which are not a matter of specific law — such as freedom to choose our own callings, freedom to quit a job and seek another, freedom to buy or not to buy, freedom for each man to venture and to protect his success, always subject to the rights of his neighbors. In short, we have freedom of choice. And the product of our freedom is the stimulation of our energies, initiative, ingenuity and creative facilities.

Freedom is the open window through which pours the sunlight of the human spirit and of human dignity. With the preservation of these moral and spiritual qualities, and with God's grace, will come further greatness for our country.

Herbert Hoover
Presidential Library

The Establishment of the Library

The complex now known as the Herbert Hoover National Historic Site and Presidential Library had its origin when Mr. Hoover visited West Branch on August 21, 1928, to begin his presidential campaign. Interest in the small cottage where he had been born began developing as of that date. In 1935 the Hoover family purchased the little house and restored it to the original site. Over the years more land was acquired and a park developed. The Hoover Birthplace Foundation, formed in 1954, took over care of the cottage and grounds. The Foundation built the Presidential Library, and on Mr. Hoover's 90th birthday, August 10, 1964, the Birthplace, Library and grounds were deeded to the Federal Government. In 1972 the Birthplace Foundation changed its name to the Hoover Presidential Library Association. The Association continues to support the Library with grants for special furnishings and educational materials.

Library Dedication

The Herbert Hoover Presidential Library was formally dedicated on Mr. Hoover's 88th birthday, August 10, 1962. It was Mr. Hoover's last public appearance. Participating in the dedication of the Library was former President Harry S. Truman. Prior to the dedication the two Presidents took a private tour of the Library, just as they had done when Mr. Hoover took part in the dedication of the Truman Library in 1957.

Portions of the Herbert Hoover Address at the Dedication of the Herbert Hoover Presidential Library at West Branch, Iowa, August 10, 1962

"I was taken from this village to the Far West 78 years ago. The only material assets which I had were two dimes in my pocket, the suit of clothes that I wore and I had some extra underpinnings provided by loving aunts.

But I carried from here something much more precious.

I had a stern grounding of religious faith.

I carried with me recollections of a joyous childhood.

And I carried with me the family disciplines of hard work . . ."

"May I say to the boys and girls of America that the doors of opportunity are still open to you. Today the durability of freedom is more secure in your country than any place in the world."

Portions of the Harry S. Truman Address at the Dedication.

"He (Mr. Hoover) did a job for me that nobody else in the world could have done. He kept millions of people from starving to death after the Second World War just as he did after the first World War . . . When I asked him if he would be willing to do the job, he never hesitated one minute. He said, 'Yes, Mr. President, I'll do it.' He did a most wonderful job of keeping these people from starving. What more can a man do?"

Archives

The Library basically serves two main functions — it is both a museum and a research center. The museum is dedicated to the presentation of the life and accomplishments of Herbert Hoover. The research center arranges and preserves a large part of his papers and some 40 other smaller manuscript collections totalling over five million items, 18,000 books, 15,000 still photographs, 70,000 feet of motion picture footage, 940 rolls of microfilm, and 175 sound recordings. All this material is made available to researchers in the Library's reading room.

Approximately 140 researchers a year visit the Library and, in addition, several hundred research requests are serviced each year through the mail. Since the Library's research center was opened in 1966, over 750 researchers have used our resources and more than 187 doctoral dissertations, 52 masters theses, 177 published volumes, and 85 articles have been researched, at least in part, at the Hoover Library.

Museum

The museum displays have been organized in a chronological arrangement and every effort has been made to make the material self-explanatory.

The museum offers various educational services for school groups throughout the year. Films are shown on a regularly scheduled basis during the summer months and upon request to groups through the remainder of the year. The staff also provides reference service and educational material by mail.

Herbert Hoover National Historic Site

The Herbert Hoover National Historic Site

The Herbert Hoover National Historic Site went through many years of planning, formulation and changes before it actually came into existence by an act of President Lyndon B. Johnson, August 12, 1965.

Work toward memorializing West Branch as the birthplace of the Thirty-First President began in 1928 when the Hoover Birthplace Committee was formed. A restoration project on the Hoover birthplace cottage began in 1938. A neighborhood of West Branch — Herbert Hoover's home as a young boy — began to be recreated as accurately as possible in the years to follow.

After restoring the birthplace

cabin, a replica of Jesse Hoover's blacksmith shop was completed, and restoration work was also accomplished on the Quaker meeting house and other historic buildings.

This section of West Branch, whose residents and general environment were so instrumental in shaping Mr. Hoover's ideals, still appears much as it did in the 1870's and 1880's.

On the ground of the 187-acre site are also found the Hoover Presidential Library-Museum, which was dedicated by Mr. Hoover in 1962. On a hillside

about a quarter-mile away from the birthplace are the graves of the President and Mrs. Hoover.

The statue of Isis, the Egyptian goddess of plenty which was given to Mr. Hoover in the 1920's by school children in appreciation of his World War I relief work, stands south of the birthplace cottage.

The Historic Site is truly a "living history" of West Branch, of the life of Mr. Hoover, and of his contributions to America and the world in the Twentieth Century.

The site has had numerous dignitaries and heads of state for formal and informal visits. Former President Dwight D. Eisenhower and former Vice President Richard M. Nixon were in attendance in 1965 for the issuance of the Herbert Hoover commemorative stamp and for the 91st birthday observance at the gravesite.

Former President and Mrs. Johnson visited the Library and historic site in 1969, as did Mamie Doud Eisenhower in 1970.

Improvements and additions to the site and its structures have been well outlined and are made only in the interest of preserving the area as it appeared a century ago.

In order to keep other buildings from crowding the site, a 30-acre scenic easement immediately west of the park was purchased by the Birthplace Foundation.

A new federal building was dedicated on the grounds in 1970. A year later the National Park Service took over administration of all buildings and grounds, except the Library-Museum.

The attempt to recreate the environment that influenced Mr. Hoover as a child is a continual process. The years to come will see more additions and improvements. But we will always have an eye on the past and the commitment of preserving a portion of history for future generations to enjoy.

Acknowledgements

*p. 17 — Reprinted with permission of TIME, The Weekly
Newsmagazine, Time, Inc., November 16, 1925.*

p. 26 — National Park Service

p. 28 — San Francisco Visitor's Bureau

p. 35 — American Red Cross

p. 49 — U.S. Army Audio-Visual Agency